Keene Valley

LIBRARY OF CONGRESS.

Chap..... Copyright No.........
Shelf....

UNITED STATES OF AMERICA.

KEENE VALLEY.

THE ADIRONDACK SERIES

WRITTEN AND ILLUSTRATED
BY
KATHERINE ELIZABETH McCLELLAN

JOHN BROWN, or *A Hero's Grave in the Adirondacks* - - 1896
KEENE VALLEY - - 1898
SARANAC LAKE (*In preparation*)
LAKE PLACID (*In preparation*)

COPYRIGHT 1898
KATHERINE ELIZABETH McCLELLAN

KEENE VALLEY

"In the Heart of the Mountains"

BY
KATHERINE ELIZABETH McCLELLAN

PUBLISHED BY THE AUTHOR
SARANAC LAKE, N. Y.

KEENE VALLEY.

KEENE VALLEY! The very name calls up memories of the most delightful drives along the river road; up and over the hills where new vistas of mountain peak and valley meadow are constantly revealed; of trips by boat through the loveliest of Adirondack waters ; of climbs, following trails to the tops of the giants which encircle the valley ; of spins along the picturesque bicycle path ; of the pleasures of trout fishing in "John's Brook," and of a wild chase over Marcy for deer.

Such memories and myriads of others may be yours, gentle reader, if this little book proves helpful to you, who are not familiar with the Valley, by suggesting its many opportunities and varied resources; and to you, who know it well, by recalling faithful pictures of what you yourself have enjoyed.

Keene Valley has long been known as the home of the artist and the haunt of the philosopher, for here nature gives with a lavish hand such a combination of wilderness and peaceful habitation as can be found nowhere else in the Adirondacks. Many men noted in art, science and philosophy come here, year after year, for inspiration and strength. The lofty peaks stand shoulder to shoulder in a long procession, stern, forbidding, rugged, and at their feet the dark Au Sable gurgles and ripples over its pebbly bed as it winds and curves, and is bordered on either side by broad and fertile meadows, with here and there a thrifty looking farm or cottage, all the picture of quiet, rural life. At the head of the Valley, and visible from almost every part of it, stands Noon Mark, so named because at noon the sun stands directly over its peculiarly shaped peak, making it a giant sun-dial, so that all the Valley folk never need miss their nooning. To the south and west, are the irregular peaks of Dix, Camel's Hump, Colvin, Resagonia, Wolf's Jaws, Gothics, Skylight, Nipple Top, Haystack and Marcy. To the east the Giant, Hopkins, Baxter and Hurricane. To the north the Cascade range, and beyond it the solitary sentinel, Whiteface, with its seared peak gleaming in the sun. Thus in every direction the mountains loom up, each with some peculiarity of form or peak, from which it usually derives its name; a

LOWER AU SABLE LAKE.

few, however, have been named for individuals, and occasionally one retains its Indian name, such as Marcy, which is so much more suggestive as Tahawus, the Cleaver of the Clouds.

The very nearness to all these giants is awe inspiring, sublime and restful. Each mountain, as you see it daily from your piazza, or get to know it more intimately by climbing its rugged sides, while always the same in form, yet ever presents new phases in its varied colorings of foliage, of shifting clouds, of glorious sunset glows.

THE HILLS

" The everlasting hills! They hedge me round,
    And hold me safe within the narrow vale.
From all the world's great turmoil not a sound
Doth penetrate these silences profound,
    Ah! Life is a paradise in this fair vale.

At morning all the east grows vivid red,
    And all the hills reflect the rosy light;
At sunset, warm and mellow rays are shed
Adown the valley, while the mountain head
    Stands for a moment bathed in glory bright.

Then like a being pure and fair as snow,
    The full moon rises grandly o'er the hills,
And mounting zenithward serene and slow,
She pours a flood of light on all below,
    And views her face in myriad mountain rills.

Ah! This is peace; to live at nature's side,
    To walk with her at morn and noon and eve,
To wander free, with nature for a guide,
To doat and dream upon life's great tide,
    To find from worldly cares a sweet reprieve "

The Valley proper has an elevation of a thousand feet, is about a half a mile wide and six miles long, all tourists and traffic pass through it, on their way to their different destinations, while those who can, linger as long as possible in this lovely spot, with its numerous attractions.

Keene Valley, with its church, post office, school-house and several well-kept stores, is a local centre. There is also a pretty little library, where an excellent variety of summer literature can be found, which was a gift to the town in 1897, and has been much appreciated, both by the townspeople and the visitors. Here are large hotels, numerous boarding houses and a number of pretty cottages to rent, besides the many summer homes, nestling along the river banks, or perched high up on the hillsides. No more beautiful spot can be found with such varied opportunities for drives, walks or climbs. A summer day can be whiled away in rest and quiet beside a mossy bank, or in a shady nook, with all the wealth of valley and mountain scenery spread out in panoramic display.

UPPER AU SABLE LAKE.

AU SABLE RIVER IN THE VALLEY.

All points can be reached from the Valley, making one's headquarters at the Adirondack House, which is centrally and delightfully situated and offers every advantage for a summer home; the principal drives can be made as half, or whole day trips, while many places are within easy walking distance. Some of those which will more than repay a visit are Mossy Cascade, Watch Rock, Sunset Rock, Phelps' Falls, Ox Bow, Washbond's Flume, Back Pasture, Young's Plateau, Hull's Falls, and Hull's Flume.

Through the whole length of the Valley runs the east branch of the Au Sable River, which has its head waters way up on the side of Marcy, and comes tumbling down through deep and narrow gorges, over steep and rocky precipices, and here and there over shallow rapids until it reaches the Valley. There it bends and curves on its winding way to Au Sable Forks, a little town some twenty miles below where it is joined by the west branch, and together they reach Lake Champlain through that wonderful chasm, The Au Sable, which is one of the natural features of Essex County.

The main road through the Valley follows the river, and is an exceedingly picturesque and beautiful drive, the more so, that it is kept in excellent condition; it is also the stage route. Stages enter the Valley from three directions; with transportation and mail to and from Westport, via Elizabethtown, twice daily; with transportation and mail to and from Au Sable Forks, once a day; also to and from Lake Placid once a day. Tourists for the Valley arrive at Westport, Au Sable Forks or Lake Placid, and enter either by the stage or by private conveyances sent out by the various hotels and boarding houses. Thus, while in the very heart of the mountains, ample opportunities and mail facilities are open for those who wish to keep in touch with the outside world.

The unique sight of a guide on a bicycle interests and delights the visitors who stay here. Nowhere else have the guides adopted the wheel, and the members of the Keene Valley Guides' Association are pioneers in this direction. One turns a second time to look at the novel picture, but the convenience and ease with which the pack and paraphernalia can be carried, prove the practical value of the adoption of the innovation. The old-time visitor to the Adirondacks finds many changes to-day, but none more startling than his Keene Valley guide on a wheel,— sure evidence of his spirit of progress.

THE VALLEY ROAD AND THE CYCLE PATH.

A KEENE VALLEY BICYCLE ASSOCIATION was formed in 1897, and by its enterprise and public spirit a charming and picturesque path has been made through the Valley, following the river road in the main; it is now possible to enjoy a spin of several miles, and no doubt the path will be improved and extended from time to time. For those who like to tramp this is a perfect paradise, well marked trails make it possible to climb nearly all the celebrated peaks, but it will always be advisable to take a guide, unless one is thoroughly familiar with the locality. A new association, known as "The Adirondack Trail Improvement Association," was formed in 1897, with the ostensible object of improving the old, and cutting new trails to peaks at present inaccessible and between various points of interest. About forty members have already been enrolled, and many new members will doubtless be added during the present season. These gentlemen are all public-spirited and enthusiastic trampers, and are anxious to add to the attraction of their summer homes, both for their own pleasure and the benefit of the many visitors who come year after year and want new worlds to conquer.

At the head of the Valley, and some two hundred and seventy-five feet above it, is an extended plateau known as Keene Heights. Here are St. Hubert's Inn and cottages and the cottages of the Adirondack Mountain Reserve, besides a number of private summer homes scattered here and there on the various knolls and points of vantage, each commanding some special view of mountain height and valley meadow. This is a charming spot, and fortunate is he who can spend his outing at St. Hubert's.

The park known as the Adirondack Mountain Reserve joins the hotel property. It is a private preserve of about forty square miles, and includes within its confines some of the loftiest mountain peaks, the beautiful Au Sable Lakes, and the waters of the Au Sable River and Gill Brook, with innumerable gorges, chasms, flumes and waterfalls. The Adirondack Mountain Reserve has built, at great expense, a beautiful drive-way from the lodge at the entrance to the Lower Au Sable Lake, a distance of three miles. A toll is charged for carriages, and the amount thus obtained is expended each year by the Association in keeping the road in condition and repair. Game and fish are also protected, but permits to fish in its waters can be had from the Superintendent, and many exciting "catches" are made each season. For it is the policy of the Association to keep its waters well stocked with trout, and to this end fry is added from year to year; no less than ten

THE ADIRONDACK HOUSE.

thousand having been put in in 1897. Game has been fully protected since the organization of the Adirondack Mountain Reserve in 1886, and no permits have as yet been granted to hunt within its limits. During the open season in the Valley the Reserve is a very haven; the hounded deer seem to know where they are safe, many run in and secure protection because of the ever watchful and tireless vigilance of the Game Warden, and it is a common occurrence when rowing up the lakes to see several deer feeding on the lily pads at their favorite haunts. In all other respects the Reserve is perfectly free to the public so long as their regulations in regard to the destruction of trees, etc., are observed. The Adirondack Mountain Reserve has never put up a special club house, but owns a number of cottages, each originally built by a member, and occupied by him. At the expiration of a given number of years and for a stipulated sum, the cottage becomes the property of the Association. Thus, while a number of the cottages are still occupied by the original owners, others have reverted to the Association and can be rented for the season. All cottages are furnished and cared for by the Association, and cooking in them is not allowed; members and guests alike taking their meals at St. Hubert's Inn. This cottage-hotel life has many charms, and solves the problem of a summer home without responsibility. New cottages are added from year to year to meet the growing demand.

THE GAME WARDEN.

The delightful walks within easy reach of St. Hubert's Inn are too many to name, but Russell Falls, Au Sable Flume, Roaring Brook Falls, Artist's Falls, Gill Brook Flume and the River Trail are a few of those which should not be missed.

Near to St. Hubert's Inn, on a sloping hillside, is the private chapel of Dr. Dubois, Felsenheim, where the Reverend Doctor holds regular services during the summer season. It is usually thronged with guests from St. Hubert's and the neighboring cottages.

A little library, known as Keene Heights Library, is also on the hotel grounds; besides well-filled shelves of the latest books, a large assortment of the daily papers and magazines are found in the reading-room. All literature pertaining to St. Hubert and the historical pictures of him are carefully preserved in their archives. The beautiful legend reads somewhat as follows: Hubert, son of Bertrande, a duke of Guienne, was a famous hunter, he was an unerring marksman, and the number and rapacity of his hunts made him

KEENE HEIGHTS LIBRARY.

FELSENHEIM.

NOON MARK FROM THE VALLEY.

KEENE VALLEY LIBRARY.

feared as well as admired. Lawless, reckless, and with never a thought for Mother Church, he was on a wild hunt in the forest of Ardennes on a certain Good Friday. Suddenly in a thicket close at hand appeared a milk white stag with a shining crucifix between his horns, and a warning voice spoke to him of his sins. He knelt in humility, was converted, and ever after became the Patron Saint of the Chase. He is said to have lived a zealous, earnest life, performing many miracles before his death, which occurred in 727. His body was placed in the Benedictine Convent of Ardain, in the Ardennes, and received the name of St. Hubert, of Ardennes.

Of the many delightful trips to be taken, it will only be possible to designate a few and indicate the others in a table of distances.

Perhaps the most pleasing of all is a trip up through the Au Sable Lakes, starting from the Adirondack House, either by private conveyance or stage,—stages run twice daily,—past St. Hubert's Inn and through the beautiful Reserve road, with glimpses of Gill Brook on the one side with its falls and flumes, and the river on the other side with its cascades and gorges. Suddenly, making a sharp turn in the road, you get a vista through the overhanging trees of the Dark Cup, as the Lower Lake is sometimes called, dark with the reflections of the lofty peaks which hem it in on either side. The beauty of these lakes beggars description; they have been variously called the "Gems of the North Woods," and the "Eyes of the Adirondacks," but it is only when seen that their beauty can be appreciated.

ST. HUBERT'S INN.

The Lower Lake, long, narrow and winding, has walls of precipitous rocks on either side which mount up and up a thousand feet from the lake, so steep and rugged that no man has ventured to climb them. Colvin is on the left, and that wonderful Indian Head, which stands like a sombre sentinel, at the entrance to the lake, and frowns down on the dark waters below.

Resagonia is on the right, with its serrated peaks, between which the Rifle Notch Pass can plainly be seen, and just to the right the Gothics appear. Leaving your horses to be cared for, and entering the boat of your guide,— all guides own their own boats,— you make the trip the length of the lake, amid the most picturesque and Swiss-like scenery; at its head you follow a trail of an easy mile along the river banks to the Upper Au Sable, a broad and placid looking lake, in striking contrast to the lower one, with sloping shores dotted here and there with rustic open camps. These camps are built and owned by the authorized guides, and each attests the ingenuity of its builder and the artistic possibilities of bark and twig.

Landing at your guide's camp, you have an hour or two for pleasurable discovery, or to watch for the expected deer, while your guide hies him to his wood-pile and kitchen. In a trice the most savory of dinners is ready,— for all the guides are excellent cooks. How appetizing it is and how delicious to eat in the open air, with the fragrant balsam and pine overhead, is proved by the surprising appetite that you have. But all too soon the

HAYSTACK AND BASIN MOUNTAINS.

COTTAGES OF THE ADIRONDACK MOUNTAIN RESERVE.

shadows begin to lengthen, and you reluctantly pack up for the return trip. Marcy, Haystack, Skylight, the Gothics and Resagonia are all mirrored in these placid waters, and if perchance there be a moon, you will have such a trip as you have never enjoyed before; the mountains seem twice their size as the black masses loom up against the moonlit sky, and the grandeur of the scene is surpassingly beautiful.

If, however, you stay several days in camp, you will be well repaid by the novel experience of such a life. For here you can row up the river to the Inlet, and by taking a short tramp on the Elk Lake trail, reach a promontory overlooking the whole Marcy range; you can climb Mt. Marcy from here by the shortest and best trail with comparative ease in a single day. Lake trout are also quite abundant in the Upper Au Sable, so that a few days in camp offer many opportunities for sport.

The East Hill drive, while rather a hard climb, is one of the trips not to be omitted. An ascent of something over a thousand feet, by a winding road, brings one to a projecting plateau; here, a little to the left and commanding a magnificent outlook, is "Summer Brook," Miss Mann's beautiful summer home, consisting of log cabin, chalet and out-buildings. "Summer Brook" is a social community, which has excited the interest of many thoughtful visitors, and presents to the casual observer at least a charming and helpful phase of community life.

Further up the mountain side can be seen "Glenmore," Prof. Davidson's Summer School of Philosophy, consisting of lecture hall, cottages and refectory; many enthusiasts assemble here annually to take the various courses of lectures on philosophy and kindred isms.

Making an abrupt turn here, around a ravine a moment later the Willey House appears. From this height the open view that one has to the south and west presents the whole valley and mountain ranges beyond in panoramic succession. Besides the magnificent view an excellent dinner can be had here, and after a rest the descent is made by another route, where new views appear, with mountain peaks hidden behind banks of fleecy clouds which usually gather in the late afternoon and reflect the glorious color of the setting sun. You reach your hotel in time for supper, and the East Hill trip remains as one of the events of the season.

For a rough, but wildly romantic drive, take the Chapel Pond Road as far as Euba Mills, going up past the great Slide and Eagle Cliffs, the Giant's Leap, or Roaring Brook Falls, the Fern Caves, and Chapel Pond itself. The Pond is a deep bowl bounded on two sides by precipitous walls of rock, weird and wild-looking. The smoke from the opposite shore gives signs of life and habitation, and here indeed is the most novel of picturesque camps, built on the shelving rocks and narrow ledge of land between the towering masses of rock

THE GIANT.

DRIVEWAY, IN RESERVE.

EAGLE CLIFFS, CHAPEL POND ROAD.

at the back and the lake shore. Several times during the season, charming fêtes or "Camp Fires" are given by the hospitable hostess, and fortunate is he who receives an invitation to these weird and beautiful sights.

Beyond Chapel Pond the road is rough and narrow, with high hills and projecting rocks on the one side and deep precipices on the other, but it is wild and beautiful. The return trip can be made from Euba Mills, or one can push on to Elizabethtown and return that night or the following day by the direct route, which is also a delightful drive, and the regular stage route between Westport and the Valley.

A delightful day excursion can be made to the Cascade Lakes. These lakes are about eleven miles from Keene Valley; taking the river road it is five miles to the foot of the big hill, here begins a steady climb of some six miles to an elevation of at least eleven hundred feet above the valley. The lakes are long and narrow, and lie in a deep ravine between Long Pond Mountain, – one of the Cascade range—and Pitch-Off. Long Pond Mountain rises abruptly from the lake shore, and there is only the width of a roadway between the lakes and Pitch-Off on the other side. It is wild and beautiful scenery, not unlike the Lower Au Sable. The lakes are very deep and black-looking, and contain quantities of brook trout ; they are the private property of the owner of the Cascade Lake House, and free to fish in, to the guests of the house, while fishing permits are granted to transients.

The geologist will find a wealth of specimens of various rare stones and gems on the mountain side near the cascade, which is a little brook that comes tumbling over Long Pond Mountain, with a fall of over eight hundred feet to the lakes below, and from which the lakes and hotel derive their name.

An excellent trout dinner can be had at the "Cascade," and the return made in the afternoon.

If, however, you care to make a two-day trip, after dinner drive to Lake Placid, nine miles, over a very good road, on the highest plateau in the Adirondacks ; to the east are Marcy, Colden and McIntyre, and straight ahead Whiteface in solitary grandeur.

Spending the night at the Ruisseaumont, Stevens House, Grand View or Lake Placid House, the return can be made the following day, with a visit to John Brown's Grave, at North Elba, as a side trip of two miles from the main road, just after you leave Lake Placid, to return to Keene Valley.

This is the veritable grave and home of John Brown, of Ossawatomie fame and Harper's Ferry martyrdom. In 1896 this historic farm was given to the state of New York, and made a part of the National Park of the Adirondacks.

Full details of John Brown and his home in the mountains, are given in "A Hero's Grave in the Adirondacks."

KEENE VALLEY FROM EAST HILL.

WHEN visiting Phelps' Falls on Prospect Hill, see Old Mountain Phelps himself, if possible. You will be interested to have a chat with the oldest guide in Keene Valley, who is also something of a philosopher and naturalist; he can appreciate the beauties of nature, especially the view from Mt. Marcy, up whose rugged sides he is said to have cut the first trail.

While the summer months offer so many attractions, yet September and October are the most beautiful of all. This is appreciated here, for the cottagers remain late and the hotels are lengthening their seasons. In the fall the mountains, which are thickly wooded, present the most glorious masses of brilliant coloring, with here and there clumps of evergreen, making a sombre setting to further enhance the yellow and red. On a frosty morning, when the crackling and snapping of the great logs in the open fire-place fills you with warmth and comfort, and you look out and see the early snows on the Giant, then, of all times of the year, do you feel the tingle of health and the buoyancy of renewed life. By ten o'clock the sun is warm and mellow and the air spicy and winey, and you are ready to enjoy a game of golf or tennis, or a brisk walk with the falling leaves rustling under foot; then Miss Louise Imogen Quincy's lines seem fitted to the scene:

> When pricks the winey air:
> When o'er the orchards clamber
> Cloud masonries of amber:
> When brooks are silver clear:
> When conquering colors dare
> The hills and craggy places
> And hold with braggart graces
> High wassail of the year:
>
> Oh! Then we knights of weather,
> Since all the birds are quiet,
> Come forth with pomp and riot,
> With trumpeting and song;
> And shout for King October!
> The blooded, bronzed October!
> The Saracen October
> To whom our swords belong.

Many guests who have spent the summer at the Saranacs or in the Lake Placid region, "drive out" by the way of Keene Valley, Elizabethtown and Westport. These places are especially beautiful at this time of year; there are so many drives about Elizabethtown that it is said, that if one stayed a month, a new drive could be taken each day. The hotels, The Windsor, The Mansion House and Maplewood Inn, all remain open for a very late season. At Westport, a beautiful, rolling country, on the shores of Lake Champlain, one lingers at the Westport Inn as long as possible, reluctant to leave and take up once again the conventionalities and social routine of metropolitan life.

"ON THE TRAIL."

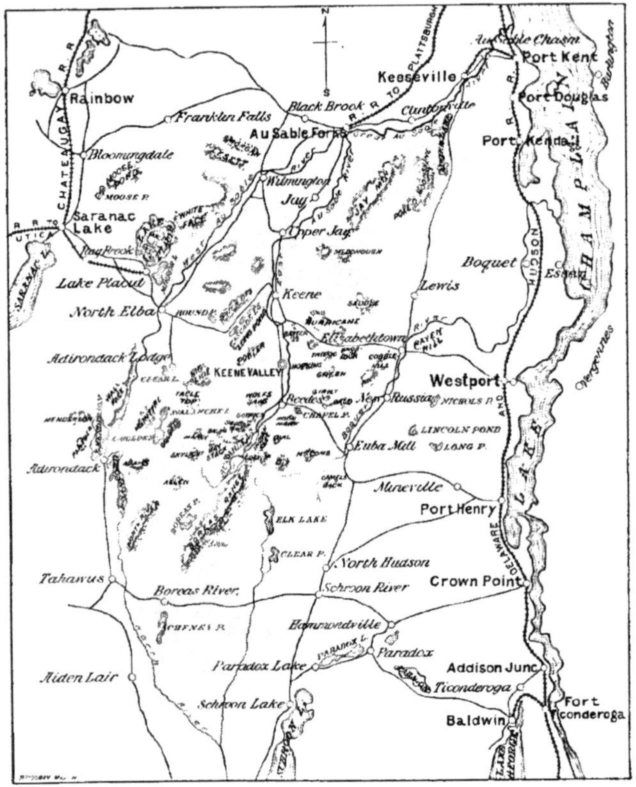

Rainbow
Bloomingdale
Franklin Falls
Black Brook
Au Sable Forks
Keeseville
Clintonville
Au Sable Chasm
Port Kent
Port Douglas
Port Kendall
Burlington
Saranac Lake
Lake Placid
North Elba
Wilmington
Jay
Upper Jay
Keene
Lewis
Boquet
Essex
Elizabethtown
Adirondack Lodge
Keene Valley
Westport
New Russia
Beedes
Euba Mill
Lincoln Pond
Long P.
Nichols P.
Vergennes
Adirondack
Mineville
Port Henry
Elk Lake
Clear P.
North Hudson
Tahawus
Boreas River
Schroon River
Crown Point
Hammondville
Paradox
Paradox Lake
Addison Junc.
Ticonderoga
Aiden Lair
Schroon Lake
Fort Ticonderoga
Baldwin
Lake George
Champlain
Delaware and Hudson R. R.
Chateaugay R. R.
R. R. to Utica
R. R. to Plattsburgh

MOUNTAINS

A list of the mountains in the vicinity of Keene Valley, with their elevations, taken from the latest U. S. Geological Survey. There are trails to the tops of nearly all of these, and registers on a number of them, put up by the Appalachian Society. For details in regard to trails and facilities for making these trips, information will be furnished by any of the authorized guides of the Valley or by applying to Mr. W. Scott Brown, Superintendent of the Adirondack Mountain Reserve.

In regard to the work contemplated by the Adirondack Trail Improvement Association, information can be had by applying to Mr. William A. White, the President, or to Mr. S. Burns Weston, the Secretary; post-office address, Beedes', Keene Heights, N. Y.

NAMES	HEIGHTS	NAMES	HEIGHTS
Basin	4,825 feet	Marcy	5,344 feet
Baxter	2,400 "	Noon Mark	3,552 "
Colvin	4,074 "	Nipple-top	4,620 "
Dial	4,023 "	Porter	4,070 "
Dix	4,804 "	Resagonia	4,138 "
Giant	4,622 "	Rooster's Comb	2,795 "
Gothics	4,738 "	Saddleback	4,530 "
Haystack	4,918 "	Skylight	4,920 "
Hopkins	3,130 "	Slide	4,255 "
Hurricane	3,087 "	Wolf's Jaws	4,225 "
Indian Head	2,500 "		

DISTANCES FROM KEENE VALLEY

A list of beautiful and desirable drives to points of interest, and their distances from Keene Valley.

NAMES	DISTANCES	NAMES	DISTANCES
Au Sable Lakes	6½ miles	Jay Village	15 miles
St. Hubert's Inn	3½ "	Au Sable Chasm	34 "
East Hill	8 "	Au Sable Forks	20 "
Chapel Pond	4½ "	Schroon Lake	32 "
Roaring Brook Falls	3 "	Lake George	50 "
Euba Mills	9 "	Cascade Lakes	11 "
High Falls (Bouquet River)	8 "	Clifford's Falls	8 "
		Adirondack Lodge	20 "
Elizabethtown	13 "	John Brown's Grave	10 "
Keene Centre	5 "	Lake Placid	20 "
Pottersville	41 "	Ray Brook	20 "
Riverside	17 "	Saranac Lake Village	30 "
Style's Falls	8 "	Saranac Lake	31 "
Underwood	10 "	Upper Saranac Lake	30 "
Westport Station	20 "	Paul Smith's	47 "
Westport Landing	21 "	Loon Lake	60 "
Port Henry	23 "	Rainbow Lake	45 "
Upper Jay	11 "	Wilmington Notch	20 "

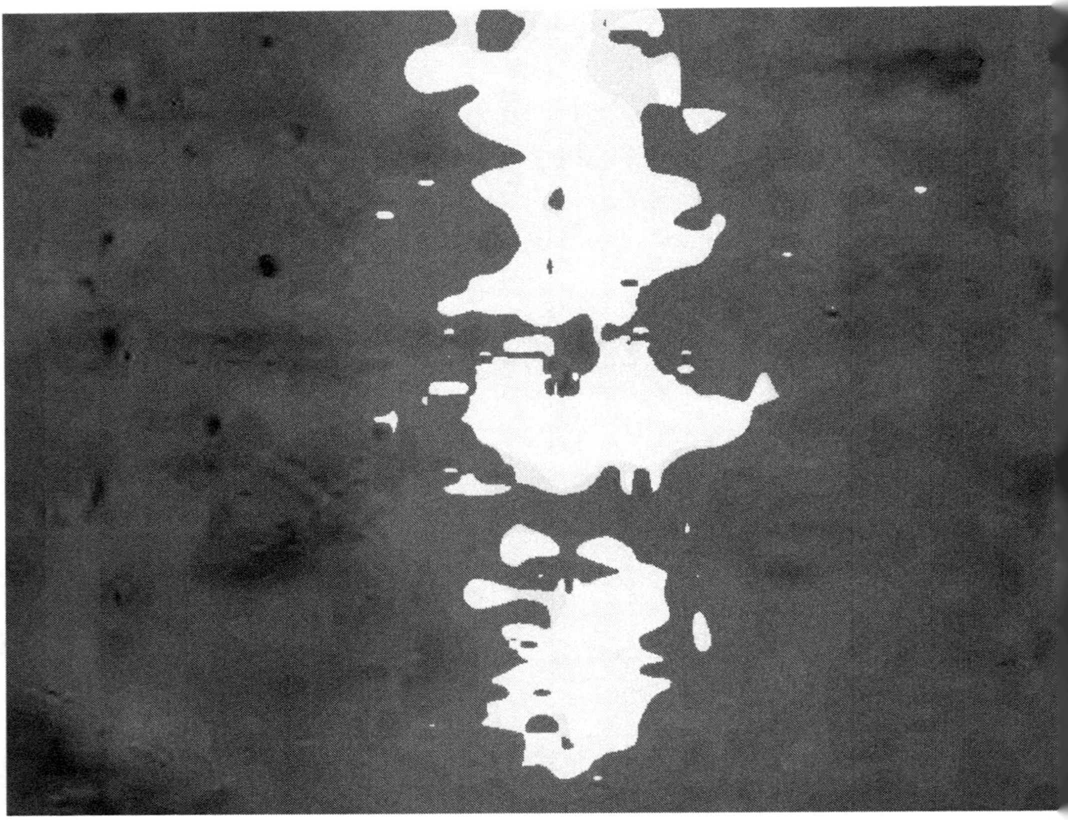